I0086690

Missions

The Chief End of the Christian Church

By Alexander Duff

PANTIANOS
CLASSICS

Published by Pantianos Classics

ISBN-13: 978-1-78987-039-8

First published in 1877

Contents

Preface...iv

Missions, the Chief End of the Christian Church..........5

Notes...28

Preface

In the spring of 1839, I happened to be appointed by the Established Presbytery of Edinburgh to preside at the ordination of the Rev. Dr. Thomas Smith, as a new missionary to India. It was on that occasion that the following discourse was delivered. Subsequently it was published in a small volume, along with the Charge and Address. That volume very rapidly passed through a number of editions; but for upwards of thirty years, it has been entirely out of print. Often has the author been solicited to bring out a new edition, but, from various causes, this has never been accomplished. Circumstances, however, connected with recent and present events, to which it is unnecessary more particularly to advert, have suggested the propriety of reprinting the discourse, as exhibiting what is believed to be a scriptural view of the subject, which has never yet been homologated by any Branch of the Reformed Church of Christendom, in a way commensurate with its transcendent importance.

Alexander Duff.
Edinburgh, 1877.

Missions, the Chief End of the Christian Church

"God be merciful unto us, and bless us; and cause His face to shine upon us. That Thy way may be known upon earth, Thy saving health among all nations."

—Psalm lxvii. 1, 2.

The royal Psalmist, in the spirit of inspiration, personating the Church of the redeemed in every age, and more especially under its last and most perfect dispensation, here offers up a sublime prayer for its inward prosperity, and outward universal extension. All is in the order of nature and of grace. Knowing full well that he who has not obtained mercy from the Lord, cannot be a fit bearer of it to others, — that he who has obtained no blessings himself, can dispense none, — that he who enjoys no light, can communicate none, — he first of all, with marked and beautiful propriety, begins with the supplication of personal and individual blessings:— 'God be merciful unto us,' forgiving and pardoning all our sins: ' and bless us,' conferring every gift and every grace really needful for time and eternity: ' and lift up the light of thy countenance upon us,' cheering us with the smile of reconciliation and love, and causing the Sun of Righteousness to arise on our darkened souls with healing in his beams.

But does the Psalmist stop here? Does he for a moment intend that he and his fellow-worshippers, as representatives of the visible Church of the living God, should absorb all the mercy, all the blessing, and all the light of Jehovah's countenance? Oh no! Having thus fervently prayed for evangelical blessings to descend upon himself, and every member of the Church, he immediately superadds, in the true evangelistic or missionary spirit, ' That thy way,' or, as it is given in our metrical version, 'That *so* thy way may be known upon *earth*, thy saving health among *all nations*.'

How significant the connection here established between the *obtainment* and the *distribution* of evangelical favours! 'God be merciful unto us, and bless us.' — Why? only that we ourselves may be pardoned and sanctified, and thereby attain to true happiness? No, There is *another grand end* in view, to the accomplishment of which our being blessed is but *a means*. 'God be merciful unto us, and bless us, *that so* thy way may be known on earth,' — that *so* — that thus — that in this way — that by our instrumentality — that by our being blessed, and having the light of thy countenance shining upon us, — ' thy way ' — thy way of justification through the atoning righteousness of the Redeemer, — thy way of sanctification by his Holy Spirit, — ' may be made known on earth, and thy saving health among *all nations*.'

And then, seized with true prophetic fire at the grandeur of the Divine design in reference to 'all nations,' and hurried away by the magnificence of the vision of the latter-day glory, does 'the sweet singer of Israel' break forth into heroic measures, sublimer far than any ever strung on Grecian or Roman lyre: —

> 'Let people praise thee, Lord;
>   Let people all thee praise:
> Oh let the nations be glad,
>   And sing for joy always.
>
> Then shall the earth yield her increase,
>   God, our God, bless us shall;
> God shall us bless, and of the earth
>   The ends shall fear Him all.'

Here the two grand characteristics of the true Church of God, — the evangelical, and evangelistic or missionary, — are written as in a sunbeam: — the evangelical, in the possession of all needful gifts and graces out of the plenitude of the Spirit's fulness: the evangelistic, in the instant and perpetual propension which that possession ought to generate and feed, instrumentally to dispense these blessings among *all nations*. As if to confound lukewarm and misjudging professors throughout all generations, these characteristics are represented by the Spirit of inspiration itself, as essential to the very existence and well-being of the Church, and in their very nature inseparable. The prayer of the Church, as dictated by the Divine Spirit, is directed to the obtainment of blessings, not as an *end, merely terminating in herself,* but as *a means* towards the promotion and attainment of an ulterior end of the sublimest description, — the enlightenment and conversion of all nations! Hence it follows, that when a Church ceases to be evangelistic, it must cease to be evangelical; and when it ceases to be evangelical, it must cease to exist as a true Church of God, however primitive or apostolic it may be in its outward form and constitution!

There is no mystery here. If, in the common affairs of life, a servant besought and obtained an increased portion of goods, that he might proceed to a distant city or foreign nation, and lay out the whole for the advancement of his master's interest; and if, instead of acting in the terms of his own requisition, and agreeably to the express design of his kind and munificent employer, he chose to remain at home, and appropriate all for his own private ends, what judgment would the world pronounce on such a man? Would he not be condemned as an unprofitable servant, who dishonestly attempted to embezzle the property of another? And would not the master be more than justified in taking away from him even all that he had?

Precisely similar is the position and attitude of the petitioning Church, and consequently, of all petitioning believers, as portrayed by the pencil of the Divine Spirit in the words of our text. Believers are there taught to pray, and all who have ever read or sung this precious psalm in a believing frame of mind have actually prayed, for the richest spiritual blessings: — what purpose? that they themselves may enjoy the comforts and consolations of piety in this life, and a meetness for the heavenly inheritance hereafter? Doubtless this is the *first end*, and must be implied and included in the object of the petition. But so little does *this* appear, in the eye of the Spirit, to be *the only* or *even the chief end*, that it is actually *left altogether unexpressed!* There is *another end* present to his omniscient view, of a nature so transcendently exalted, that the former is, as it were, wholly overlooked, because eclipsed by the surpassing glory of that which excelleth. And that other end of all-absorbing excellence is, *the impartation of God's saving health to all nations.* So pre-eminent in importance does this end appear to the mind of the Spirit, that believers are taught to implore spiritual blessings, expressly, and even chiefly, that they may thereby have it in their power the more effectually to promote it throughout the world!

If, then, in answer to *such* prayers, spiritual blessings should be conferred from on high; and if, instead of employing them for the promotion of their Divine Master's interest, by causing his saving health to be made known to all nations, believers should sit down in ease, and appropriate all to themselves, and their own friends immediately around them, — what judgment must be pronounced upon them in the court of heaven? Must they not be condemned as guilty of a breach of faith — guilty of a dereliction of duty to their Lord and Master — guilty of a dishonest attempt to embezzle the treasures of his grace? And if so, must not their sin, if unrepented of, bring down its deserved punishment? And what can the first drop from the vial of Divine wrath do less, than expunge from the spiritual inventory of such worthless stewards, all that they have already so gratuitously and undeservedly obtained? What a resistless argument does the Spirit of God here supply in favour of the missionary enterprise! Who can peruse the words of his own inspiration, without being overwhelmed with the conviction that, in his unerring estimate, j j the chief end for which the Church ought to exist — the chief end for which individual church-members ought to live, is the evangelization or conversion of the world? [1]

But lest any shade of dubiety should exist as to the incontrovertible legitimacy of this conclusion, the same

momentous truth may be established by other and independent evidence. The spirit of prophecy, speaking
through Isaiah, had long announced the Messiah Himself,
not only as King and Priest, but as the *great Prophet and
Evangelist of the world*. 'The Spirit of the Lord is upon me',
says the Divine Oracle, 'because the Lord hath appointed
me to preach good tidings to the meek: he hath sent me to
bind up the broken-hearted, to proclaim liberty to the
captives, and the opening of the prison to them that are
bound; to proclaim the acceptable year of the Lord; to
appoint unto them that mourn in Zion, to give unto them
beauty for ashes, the oil of joy for mourning, the garment
of praise for the spirit of heaviness.' And lest any might
suppose that the exercise of the functions here described
was to be limited to the Jews, the *natural seed* of Abra-
ham, God's chosen people; or the Zion here named was
meant exclusively to denote the *literal local Zion* at Jerusalem, and not rather, in type and figure, the true Catholic
Church throughout the world, — it is almost immediately
added, 'For Zion's sake will I not hold my peace, and for
Jerusalem's sake will I not rest, until the righteousness
thereof go forth as brightness, and the salvation thereof
as a lamp that burneth: and the *Gentiles* shall see Thy
righteousness, and *all* kings Thy glory.' The prophetic im-
port and design of these words can admit of no doubt. For
when, on one occasion, our blessed Saviour stood up in
the Synagogue, and, opening the book of the Prophet
Esaias, read the former of these passages, he distinctly
appropriated the application of it to himself, saying, 'This
day is this Scripture fulfilled in your ears.'

Again, if it was prophesied that the Messiah would '
raise up the tribes of Jacob, and restore the prescribed of
Israel,' it is immediately added, 'I will also give thee for a

light to the *Gentiles,* that thou mayest be my salvation to *the ends of the earth.'* And again, ' Men shall be blessed in him; *all nations* shall call him blessed.'

In strict accordance, not only with the substance, but almost the *very words* of these and many other prophecies, we find the announcement of the heavenly host to the shepherds of Bethlehem: ' Behold, I bring you *good tidings* of great joy, which shall be to *all people*; for unto you is born this day a *Saviour,* which is Christ the Lord.' — The introductory salutation of the Baptist, the Messiah's forerunner: ' Behold the Lamb of God, which taketh *away the sin of the world!* — And, lastly, the solemn declaration of the Apostle John: ' In him was life, and the life was the *light of men.* That was *the true light* which *lighteth every man that cometh into the world.'*

Now, during our Saviour's ministry, he conveyed many significant intimations to his disciples that he intended to transfer to them, and through them to the body of believers in every age, those high functions which *primarily* and rightfully belonged to himself as the world's Evangelist. 'Ye are,' said he, 'the salt,' not of Judea or Jerusalem, but *'of the earth'* One of the brightest of his own prophetic titles was, 'the light of the Gentiles;' or, in the paraphrase of the Apostle, ' the light that lighteth every man that cometh into the world.' And this very title he transfers to his disciples, saying, *'Ye are the light,'* not of Judea or Jerusalem, but *'of the world.'* [2]

And, when about to withdraw his visible presence from the earth, he *formally* transferred the *whole* of his *visible evangelistic* functions to his professing disciples or Church, to be exercised and administered by it, in his name and stead, till the end of time. *'All power',* said he, *'is given unto me in heaven and in earth. Go ye, therefore,* and teach *all* nations, baptizing them in the name of the Father, and of the Son, and of the Holy Ghost — teaching them (*i.e. all* nations) to observe all things whatsoever I have commanded you; and lo! I am with *you alway, even unto the end of the world.*'

This is the grand charter under which a visible Church, directly holding of its Divine Head, was at first constituted, and designed to be for ever perpetuated, for the administration of Gospel ordinances, and the exercise of spiritual authority. These high functions in the Royal Head were original and underived, — as transferred to his body, the Church, they are, of necessity, derivative and vice-regal.   As Christ, therefore, was proclaimed by prophets and apostles, as well as by himself, in his appropriation of prophetic announcements, to be the world's Evangelist; — in his personal absence during the present dispensation, he was pleased solemnly to appoint and constitute the Church to be his *delegated representative* as the world's evangelist; and, along with the evangelistic functions, he conveyed the *power* and *authority* indispensable for their exercise.

That this was the interpretation put upon this *original Gospel commission* by the primitive disciples, is evident, not only from the whole tenor of their conduct, but also from the most express declarations scattered throughout the Book of the Acts, as well as the Apostolic Epistles.

It thus appears abundantly manifest, from multiplied Scripture evidence, that the *chief end* for which the Christian Church is constituted — the *leading design* for which she is made the repository of heavenly blessings — the *great command* under which she is laid — the *supreme function* which she is called on to discharge — is, in the name and stead of her glorified Head and Redeemer, unceasingly to act the part of an evangelist to *all the world*. The inspired prayer which she is taught to offer for spiritual gifts and graces, binds her, as the *covenanted condition on which they are bestowed at all,* to dispense them to *all nations.* The divine charter which conveys to her the warrant to teach and preach the Gospel at all, binds her to teach and preach it to *all nations.* The divine charter which embodies a commission to administer Gospel ordinances at all, binds her to administer these to *all nations.* The divine charter which communicates power and authority to exercise rule or discipline at all, binds her to exercise these not alone or exclusively, to secure her own internal purity and peace, union and stability; but chiefly and supremely, in order that she may thereby be enabled the more speedily, effectually, and extensively, to execute her grand evangelistic commission in preaching the Gospel to *all nations.*

If, then, any body of believers, united together as a Church, under whatever form of external discipline and polity, do, in their individual, or congregational, or corporate national capacity, wilfully and deliberately overlook, suspend, or indefinitely postpone, the accomplishment of the *great end* for which the Church universal, including every evangelical community, implores the vouchsafement of spiritual treasures — the *great end* for which she has obtained a separate and independent constitution at all, — how can they, separately or conjointly, expect to realize, or realizing, expect to render abiding, the promised presence of Him who alone hath the keys of the golden treasury, and alone upholds the pillars of the great spiritual edifice? If any Church, or any section of a Church, do thus neglect the *final cause* of its being, and violate the very condition and tenure of all spiritual rights and privileges, how can it expect the continuance of the favour of Him from whom alone, as their Divine fount and spring-head, all such rights and privileges must ever flow? And if deprived of His favour and presence, how can any Church expect long to *exist,* far less spiritually to flourish, in the enjoyment of inward peace, or the prospect -of outward and more extended prosperity?

And what is the whole history of the Christian Church but one perpetual proof and illustration of the grand posi-tion, — *that an evangelistic or missionary Church is a spir-itually flourishing Church; and, that a Church which drops the evangelistic or missionary character, speedily lapses into superannuation and decay!*

The most evangelistic period of the Christian Church was, beyond all doubt, the primitive or apostolic. Then, the entire community of saints seemed to act under an overpowering conviction of their responsible duty, as the divinely appointed evangelists of a perishing world. No branch or off-set from the apostolic stock at Jerusalem had, in those days, begun to surmise that, not only its first, but chief, and almost exclusive duty, was to witness for Christ in the city, or district, or province, or kingdom, in which it was itself already planted; — in other words, to surmise, that the most effectual mode of vindicating its title to the designation of apostolic, was to annihilate its own apostolicity! For what can be named, as the *most pe-culiar and distinguishing* feature in the apostolic Church at Jerusalem, if not the burning and the shining aspect of salvation which it held forth towards *all nations?* No, no. In those days, the Church's prayer, as breathed by the in-spired Psalmist, seemed to issue from every lip, and kin-dle every soul into correspondent action. The Redeemer's parting command seemed to ring in every ear, and vitally influence every feeling and faculty of the renewed soul. Every man and woman, and almost every child, through the remotest branches of the wide-spreading Church, seemed impelled by a holy zeal to discharge the functions of a missionary. All, all seemed moved and actuated towards a guilty and lost world, as if they really felt it to be as much their duty to disseminate the Gospel among unchristianized nations, as to pray, or teach, or preach to those within the pale of their respective Churches, — as much their duty to propagate the knowledge of salvation among the blinded heathen, as to yield obedience to any commandment in the Decalogue. And were not those the days of flourishing Christianity? Has not the spiritual beauty and brightness of the primitive Church been the theme of admiration and praise to succeeding generations? But no sooner did the Church, in any of its subdivisions, begin to contract the sphere of its efforts in diffusing abroad the light of the everlasting Gospel, — no sooner did it begin to settle down with the view of snugly enjoying the glorious prerogatives conferred by its Great Head, — forgetful of the multitudes that were still famishing for lack of knowledge, to all of whom it was bound by covenant to announce the glad tidings of salvation: — in a word, no sooner did the Church, in contravention of Heaven's appointed ordinance, begin to relax in the exercise of its evangelistic function towards the world at large, than its sun, under the hiding of Jehovah's countenance, and the frown of his displeasure, began to decline [3] and hide itself amid the storms of wrathful controversy, or sink beneath a gloomy horizon laden with freezing rites and soul-withering forms.

It may be thought that the history of the Reformation tends to contradict this general view. So far from this, it is to that very period, as compared with the times immediately succeeding, that we would appeal for one of the most striking illustrations of its truth. Doubtless the Pagan world was not included within the immediate sphere of the Reformers' labours. Its miserable condition was then scarcely, if at all, known in its real horror; the very existence of the great Western Continent was but recently discovered; and, in comparison with present times, the facilities of intercommunion with distant parts of the globe were so circumscribed as to appear to us hardly conceivable.

Still, the work of the Reformation was itself a grand evangelistic work. God, by his Spirit, put it into the hearts of an enlightened few to arise and make an ' aggressive movement ' on the unenlightened many, by whom they were everywhere surrounded. Their first and paramount object was to rescue the Bible itself — the great instrument of the world's evangelization — from the dormitory of dead and unintelligible languages; to emancipate its doctrines from the superincumbent load of Popish traditions and Aristotelian subtleties; to vindicate the rights of conscience in the perusal and interpretation of that Magna Charta of all civil and religious liberty; and, finally, to bring out, and separate from idolatrous Rome, a true Church, that might for ever *protest* against all doctrines and rites whatsoever, that infringed, by one jot or tittle, on Christ's supremacy, as the sole and all-sufficient Saviour of lost sinners, — a witnessing Church, that might reassume the great evangelistic function of preaching the Gospel *as a testimony to all nations.*

This struggle with anti-Christian Rome was, indeed, a long and terrible one, — a struggle which, as regards the extent of the field, the might of the combatants, the imperishable interests contended for, and the momentous consequences dependent thereon, has no parallel in history, except the dreadful conflict of primitive Christianity with Pagan Rome. But if the struggle was tremendous, proportionally glorious was the issue.

Look at the Protestant Church of this land at the close of the Reformation era. It would seem as if the very windows of heaven had then opened, and the showers of grace had descended in an inundation of spiritual gifts and graces, converting the parched lands into pools of water, and the barren wilderness into gardens that bloomed and blossomed as the rose.

Look at the same Church in less than a generation afterwards. What a poor, torpid, shrunken, shrivelled thing! As if the heavens were of brass, and the earth of iron, and no dew descending, the very waters of the sanctuary became stagnant, and bred and sent forth a teeming progeny of heresies, schisms, and dissents. Ah, how is the beauty of Israel effaced in our high places! How are the mighty fallen! Whence the cause of so sad a discomfiture?

'It was not in the battle;
No tempest gave the shock.'

No: — it was the blight and mildew of Jehovah's displeasure, on account of a neglected and unfaithful stewardship!

The *active principle* in man, which, though often sluggish, and oftener still strangely misdirected, is never wholly extinguished, was aroused by the Reformation into unwonted energy. And most legitimately was it then made to expend its force, in the awful struggle with anti-Christian Rome. But, on the total cessation of hostilities, and the restoration of general peace, how ought the awakened energy of the Reformed Church to have been directed and expended? Plainly, and incontrovertibly, it ought to have found its constant and determinate object — its divinely intended employ — in extending the triumphs of Protestant, that is, primitive, Christianity over the realms of Paganism. But, instead of this, the Church, soon casting aside her weapons of aggressive warfare, settled down, in inglorious ease, to enjoy the conquests she had won. What then? Did her active energy abate or sink into torpid quiescence? No: as a proper outlet was denied to it, in assaulting the enemy *without,* it recoiled, with a vehement rebound, on the heads of the negligent and slothful *within.* That mighty force which should have been rightfully exerted in demolishing the heathenism of the nations, soon found ample vent for itself in fomenting intestine discords and unhallowed speculation, idle impertinences and heretical controversy, — thus proving, when left undirected to its proper object, through lukewarmness and treasonable neglect, at once the scourge of the faithless professor, and the unhappy instrument of the Church's distraction and decay.

We have comparatively little or no guilt in this respect, to charge home upon the Reformers. The great work assigned to them by heaven, they executed in a manner that far exceeds 'all Greek, all Roman fame.' It is at the door of their successors — for whom the battle had been fought, and the victory won — that the blame must be laid, for which we can find no palliation.

When, after the Reformation, the Protestant Church arose, as by a species of moral resurrection, with newborn energies, from the deep dark grave of Popish ignorance and superstition, — then was she in an attitude to have gone' forth in the spirit of her own prayers, and, in obedience to the Divine command, on the spiritual conquest of the nations, — and, in the train of every victory, scatter as her trophies, the means of grace, and as her plentiful heritage, the hopes of a glorious immortality. But instead of thus fulfilling the immutable law of her constitution [4] — instead of going forth in a progress of *outward* extension and onward aggression, with a view to consummate the great work which formed at once the eternal design of her Head, and the chief end of her being, — the Church seemed mainly intent on turning the whole of her energies *inward* on herself. Her highest ambition and ultimate aim seemed to be, to have herself begirt as with a wall of fire that might devour her adversaries — to have her own privileges fenced in by laws and statutes of the realm — to have her own immunities perpetuated to posterity by solemn leagues and covenants.

All well, admirably well, had she only borne distinctly in mind that she was thus highly favoured, not for her own sake *alone,* but that, by her instrumentality, the glad tidings of salvation, through a crucified Redeemer, might be made known to *the uttermost ends of the earth.* All well, admirably well, had she only borne in mind that her candlestick was not rekindled *solely* for her own use, — but that the light of the Gospel might largely emanate therefrom, and be diffused throughout *the nations.* All well, admirably well, had she only borne in mind that she possessed no *exclusive* proprietary right to the blessings of the covenant of grace, — but that, like every other branch of the true Church of Christ, she held these in commission for the benefit of a *whole world* lying in wickedness. Ah, had the Church of these lands, in the day of her glorious triumph and *undivided* strength, gone forth

19

in accordance with the *letter* and *spirit* of her own heaven-inspired prayers, — as the Almoner of Jehovah's bounties to a perishing world, — how different might have been her position now! Instead of being compelled to act on the defensive, — instead of being reduced to the necessitous condition of a besieged city, around which the enemy is drawing his lines of circumvallation, threatening to demolish her towers, dismantle her bulwarks, and erase her palaces, — leaving her brave sons no alternative but that of raising the desperate war-cry of beleaguered valour, 'No surrender! No surrender!' — she might all along have been acting on the offensive, against 'principalities and powers, and spiritual wickednesses in high places.' And, after having made the circuit of the globe, she might this day have been displaying her standard, engraven with a thousand victories, in front of some of the last strongholds of heathenism, and rending the air with the conqueror's shout of 'Unconditional submission!'

Is it, then, too late to retrieve our past errors and criminal neglect? No: blessed be God, it is not yet too late. In answer to the prayers of a faithful remnant in this land, the Lord hath been pleased once more to regard with special favour that branch of the Holy Catholic Church to which we more immediately belong. [5] He hath been pleased to look down from heaven, and visit this his vine, and the vineyard which his own right hand once planted. And now, if ever, is the time to exhibit, not only the model of a Gospel Church, hut a complete model in full operation. We are placed in very different circumstances from those of the early Reformers. We have not, like them, to begin anew. We have not, like them, to reckon up our Protestants by units. We have not, like them, to struggle on for years in attempting to new-create, as it were, a true Church from the dark womb of Popish superstition. We have not, like them, to resist unto blood for many years more in establishing the platform of a pure ecclesiastical constitution. No. We at once count our hundreds of thousands of members united together as a Church, under one of the noblest, and purest, and most apostolic constitutions which the world has ever seen. We have the entire machinery ready-made. We have only to arise, and, in the strength of our God, set all the parts of it in motion, — and thus, at once, and simultaneously, discharge all the functions, not merely of an evangelic, but of an evangelistic Church.

That Church, which, notwithstanding many acknowledged weaknesses, and even alleged deformities, must be regarded as our venerable parent still, may already have passed through the different stages of existence. From the feebleness of infancy, she may have speedily risen to the giant vigour of maturity, — and, passing the meridian of her power, may at length have sunk enervated under a load of years. But. what of all this, if, in answer to the prayer, ' Come from the four winds, breath, and breathe upon these dry bones, that they may live,' — we behold everywhere a moving and a shaking amongst them? And if, already, we behold her beginning to exhibit cheering symptoms of a revival, — to exchange the hoariness and withered features of age, for the greenness and blooming freshness of youth; — if, by the new quickening of all her powers, she has now resolved to roll back the dark tide of corruption, which is said to have swollen to mountainous height with the lapse of time; and begun to emulate the purity and ardour of her Reformation faithfulness, — oh! let her not again be guilty of committing the egregious, the fatal, and it may be, the irremediable blunder and sin of attempting to grasp and appropriate all religious rights, blessings, and privileges; as if these were a *special monopoly,* exclusively intended for herself and her children, and not rather, what they truly are in the Divine purpose and design, a *sacred deposit,* committed to her for the enriching of the famished nations! On the contrary, let her new-burnish all the lamps of her noble institutions: let her add to these by hundreds, — not to dispel the darkness within her own territory alone, but for the kindling of a flame that shall rise, and spread, and brighten, till it illumine the world. Let her revive the golden age of the Christian Church, when professing believers, not satisfied with showers of words that contrast so ominously with barren practices, were ever prepared to testify, not only the sincerity, but the height and depth, and length and breadth of their gratitude and love to the blessed Redeemer, by submitting to the amplest sacrifices of comfort, and life, and all; — when the Christian treasury was replenished to overflowing by the free-will offerings of a self-denying, God-honouring people; — and when a general assembly of apostles and prophets met at Jerusalem, to select and set apart, not the young and inexperienced, but the greatest and most redoubted champions, to go forth and shake the strongholds of error to their basis, by sounding the Gospel trump of jubilee. Let the Protestant Church of these lands, in this the day of her incipient revival, thus nobly resolve to assume the entire evangelistic character, and implement the Divine condition of preservation and prosperity, by becoming the dispenser of Gospel blessings, not only to the people at home, but as speedily as possible, to all the unenlightened nations of the earth. And, if there .be truth in the Bible, — if there be certainty in Jehovah's promises, — if there be reality in past history ,r — she may yet arise and shine, fair as the moon, bright as the sun, and terrible as an army with banners.

Again, we say, the field of Divine appointment is not Scotland or England, but *'the world'*, — the world of 'all nations.' The prayer of Divine inspiration is, 'God bless and pity us' — not, that thy way may be known in all Britain, and thy saving health among all its destitute families, — but, ' that thy way may be known on all *the earth*, and thy saving health among *all nations.'* The command of Divine obligation is not, 'Go to the people of Scotland, or of England,' but, ' Go into *all the world*, and preach the Gospel to *every creature.'* And if we take our counsel from those blind and deluded guides, that would, in spite of the Almighty's appointment, and in derision of our own prayers, persuade us, altogether, or for an *indefinite* period onwards, to abandon the real proper Bible field, and direct *the whole* of our time, and strength, and resources to *home:* if, at their anti-scriptural suggestions, we do thus dislocate the Divine order of proportion: if we do thus invert the Divine order of magnitude: if we daringly presume to put that last, which God hath put first: to reckon that least which God hath pronounced greatest: what can we expect but that he shall be provoked, in sore displeasure, to deprive us of the precious deposit of misappropriated grace, and inscribe ' Ichabod ' on all our towers, bulwarks, and palaces? And if He do, — then, like beings smitten with judicial blindness, we may hold hundreds of meetings, deliver thousands of speeches, and publish tens of thousands of tracts, and pamphlets, and volumes, in defence of our chartered rights and birthright liberties; — and all this we may hail as religious zeal, and applaud as patriotic spirit. But if such prodigious activities be designed solely, or even chiefly, to concentrate all hearts, affections, and energies, on the limited interests of our own land: if such prodigious activities recognise and aim at no higher terminating object than the simple maintenance and extension of our home institutions, — and that, too, for the exclusive benefit of our own people, — while, in contempt of the counsels of the eternal, the hundreds of millions of a guilty world are coolly abandoned to perish: — oh! how can all this appear in the sight of heaven as anything better than a national outburst of monopolising selfishness? And how can such criminal disregard of the Divine ordinance, as respects the evangelisation of a lost world, fail, sooner or later, to draw down upon us the most dreadful visitation of retributive vengeance?

Thus it was with the Jews of old. Twice, after the creation and the flood, was the true religion universal; and if, subsequently, it contracted in its sphere, and shut up within the narrow bounds of a favoured locality, it was out of mercy and lovingkindness to man. It was, that it might not be wholly swept away and lost in the swelling tide of an apostasy, which threatened to rise and overwhelm all the kindreds of the nations. But, in the Eternal decree, it was ordained — and by the mouth of prophets who spoke in successive ages, as they were moved by the Holy Ghost, it was clearly foretold that, in the fulness of time, the true religion should once more become universal — that out of Jerusalem the law should go forth to *the ends of the earth*. The inhabitants of Jerusalem, however, resolved that beyond the bounds of Judea, their own beloved home, it should not go, — and thus dared the Omnipotent to hostile collision. And never, never did any people put forth efforts, of a nature so absolutely volcanic, in defence of their heaven-ordained institutions. But it was all in order that they might wholly monopolize the advantages of these to themselves. Calamitous monopoly! Insane opposition! Preservation of the types and shadows for their own exclusive benefit, was the Jewish watch-word. Preservation of the substance in new, extended, and remodelled forms for the benefit of the 'world,' was the Divine watchword. Who could for a moment doubt which must in the end prevail? Surely the people that could presume to contend, in unequal strife, with the full thunder of Jehovah's power, must have been more than ordinarily infatuated? And seized they verily were with a *judicial* infatuation, out of which they were not, and would not, be awakened till the tempest of Divine wrath burst upon them with exterminating violence!

And thus, assuredly, will it be with us, if we do not arise, and speedily resolve to discharge *all* those high catholic and evangelistic functions that devolve upon us, as a Protestant Church and Protestant nation. Or, shall we blindly and perversely determine, alike to scorn the counsels of heaven, and brave the warnings of Providence? Then let us only try the fatal, the disastrous experiment! — let us try, if we will, and overlook wholly, or in great measure, heaven's irrevocable law, and our own plighted obligations to save a lost world, — let us try, if we will, and maintain the warfare in defence of our home institutions, altogether or chiefly, for our own benefit and that of our children, — and as sure as Jehovah's purposes are unchangeable, our doom is sealed. By unparalleled exertions, we may arrest, for a season, the day of national calamity. We may retard, but shall not be able finally to arrest, the progress of national disorganization and decay. The chariot wheels of destruction may be made to drag more heavily as they roll along the fatal declivity.

25

But nothing, nothing shall effectually prevent the ultimate awful plunge of all our institutions - social, civil, and religious, - into the troubled waters, where they shall be dashed to pieces, amid rocks and quicksands, in a hurricane of anarchy!

To avert a catastrophe so fell and so terrible, oh! let us all imbibe into our inmost souls the Church's heaven-inspired prayer — 'Lord bless and pity us, shine on us with Thy face.' In order to prove the sincerity wherewith the prayer is uttered, let us put forth the mightiest exertions in the endeavour to repair all the ancient channels, and open up hundreds of new ones, through which the blessing may be expected to descend, in refreshing streams, into every congregation, every household, and every heart in our own land. But oh! let us not, in blind, and narrow-minded, and anti-Christian selfishness, forget the *final cause* and *chief end* for the furtherance of which, the blessing must be mainly sought by us, and for the accomplishment of which, it must be mainly conferred, if conferred at all, by a gracious God, — as emphatically taught us in the ever memorable words of his own Holy Spirit, 'That *so* thy way may be known upon *earth,* and thy saving health among *all nations.'* And let not our efforts in attempting to realize the glorious end for which evangelical mercies and favours are avowedly sought and bestowed be either feeble or disproportionate, — lest, by deficient or contradictory practices, our prayers should prove so many idle mockeries of our God; and our petitions, so many provocations to the High and Holy One, to withdraw from us altogether those privileges which we already enjoy, — if we enjoy them only with the selfish and dishonest intention of enriching ourselves by defrauding the world.

Come and let us, with united heart and soul, adopt as our own, the fervid language of one who drank deep at the fount of inspiration, — one, whose presence once gladdened these shores, and tended to chase the darkness from heathen lands, — one, who is now of the happy number of glorified spirits that cease not to chant their hallelujahs before the throne. And, while we appropriate his glowing words as the vehicle of our own irrepressible longings, — oh! let our hands be ever ready to give prompt effect to the utterance of the heart, when we sing, —

'Waft, waft, ye winds, his story,
    And you, ye waters roll;
Till, like a sea of glory.
    It spread from pole to pole:
Till o'er our ransomed nature,
    The Lamb for sinners slain,
Redeemer, King, Creator,
    In bliss return to reign.'

Notes

[1] When strongly urging the claims of the world on the Christian Church, we are constantly met with language to this effect: — By causing the mental eye to dilate itself over the grand and the magnificent, are you not apt to overlook and despise the useful and the practicable? By no means. To every church, congregation, and individual member, the heavenly monition is still addressed, ' What thy hand findeth to do, do it with all thy might,' — in whatever sphere Providence may have appointed your lot; but in so doing, never for a moment lose sight of the grand ulterior object for which the Church was originally constituted, and spiritual rights and privileges conferred, viz. the conversion of the world. By the encouragements of Scripture prophecies, — by the specific appropriation and use of Scripture petitions, — by the binding obligation of Divine commands, — you are bound to pray and to labour for the conversion of a lost world. The amount and direction of your actual exertions in the great cause, must of necessity vary with varying abilities, and means and opportunities of usefulness, and a thousand providential contingencies; but your eye must ever be fixed on the accomplishment of the great design, as the proper terminating object. In immediate and simultaneous action you may not, you cannot, be a cosmopolite; but in spirit, and prayer, and longing, and positive appetency, a cosmopolite you may, and ought to be. In primitive times, when the Divine command was still sounding in the ears of those who first received it, by extraordinary vision and otherwise, it was directly signified to holy apostles that the ' set time ' to favour one particular nation had not yet come, while a door, large and effectual, was shown to be opened in another. With such supernatural intimations, the

Church cannot now expect to be privileged; but by due attention to the leadings of Providence, the same end may be inferentially obtained. Should one nation be hermetically sealed against missionary operations, by temporary impracticability of access, or savage decrees of exterminating intolerance, — what is this but the voice of Providence distinctly proclaiming, that the set time for favouring that nation has not yet come? Should another nation be manifestly thrown open, and facilities for diffusing the gospel therein abundantly multiplied, what is this but the finger of Providence directing the Church to enter in and take possession of the land? But, in proceeding to cultivate the open and accessible, we must not forget the closed and the inaccessible, — we must pray most earnestly that all impediments may be speedily removed; and when removed, we must labour that the Gospel may have free course and be glorified, till at length it overspread the globe. This, this is the grand end towards which all our prayers and plans for the extension of Christ's Church ought directly or proximately to point, — and in its full accomplishment and that alone, be made to terminate. Like the conductors of a new colony, who are laid under imperative obligation to bring all the tracts of a district into cultivation, as the sole condition of being allowed to retain permanent possession of any, the disciples of Jesus may first commence with the most facile spots, and, converting these into advanced posts, proceed to the less tractable, — terminating at last with the least tractable of all. But should they lose sight of the ultimate end, and wilfully or indolently stop short of its accomplishment, do they not plainly incur a forfeiture of what they have already acquired? The field for Christian husbandry is the world, — and nothing short of its universal cultivation will suit the Divine design, or implement the obligations of the Christian Church.

[2] In the Bible, almost all visible objects are consecrated as significant types of invisible realities. The grand natural type of Christ is the sun; and of his Church the moon. The sun shines with a created light of its own: Christ, in his essential

divinity, has ever shone in his own uncreated light. The moon has no light of her own, and is luminous only from reflecting the rays of the natural sun: The Church has no light of her own, and shines only by reflecting the beams of the spiritual sun — the great Sun of Righteousness. The grand ordinance of the moon is, during the temporary absence of the sun, to cast its borrowed and mellow lustre over the benighted world of material forms: The grand ordinance of the Church is, during the personal absence of her Divine Head, to spread her borrowed and softened radiance over the benighted world of spiritual being. When the king of day bursts from his chambers in the east, rejoicing as a strong man to run his race, the moon may well drop her enlightening functions in the presence of his surpassing brightness: and when the King of Glory issues forth from his royal chambers in the heaven of heavens to assume, in visible manifested forms, the reins of universal government, the Church may then, but not till then, resign her delegated functions in illumining a darkened world, — because then her feeble light must be swallowed up and lost in the effulgence of his glory.

[3] 'Its sun began to decline,' etc. The Christian reader need scarcely be reminded, that at no period had the light and life of Christianity become wholly extinct. In the history of the Church, days of glorious sunshine are seen to alternate with nights of gloomiest darkness. Even in the longest and darkest night, that of the Middle Ages, we find many a lamp twinkling athwart the gloom. At length the Reformation burst upon the world with somewhat of the effulgence of primitive Christianity. And, on a review of nearly eighteen centuries and a-half, it may perhaps be affirmed, that the history of the Church has been marked with ' an obvious and triumphant progress ' on the whole. On this subject there are some compact and beautifully-expressed remarks, in the introduction to a recent publication, entitled *'History of Revivals of Religion in the British Isles, especially in Scotland.'* It is a work which ought to be found on the study-table of every clergyman. Besides the his-

torical matter, the work abounds with original reflections characterized by such energy of thought and expression, and withal such fervent piety, as to prove that the authoress might, if she willed, become the Hannah More of Scotland. Why does she not cast aside the *anonymous* veil, and by her publications, at once assume the character of open and avowed authorship?

[4] This is said in perfect knowledge of what has been recently recorded respecting occasional bursts of benevolence, on the part of the Church, in sending pecuniary relief to poor and suffering Protestants on the Continent; as well as occasional gleams and glimpses of still higher duties, in sending the Gospel to the unenlightened abroad, and more especially in the British colonies and dependencies. To all this it is perfectly just and proper to appeal, when repelling the ungenerous and unfounded attacks of those who would represent the Protestant Church of these lands as having been, throughout, wholly, and absolutely, and irredeemably negligent in the exercise of *every* function and the discharge of *every* duty; and when parrying the assaults of those who may belong to communities that *never did anything at all* in the way of foreign benevolence. But it were a perfect caricature of our Saviour's missionary design — a perfect parody of the Church's evangelistic duty — to maintain that any one, or all of these partial and isolated acts, amounted, by the slightest degree of approximation, to that sustained, enlarged, and systematic effort for the conversion of the heathen world, which alone is entitled to the name of the missionary enterprise.

[5] From the peculiar object of the services of the day, the preacher was naturally led to refer more particularly to that branch of the Church Universal of which he was a member. But all the *general* principles involved in his remarks, must at once be seen to be alike applicable to every other section of the great Protestant community.

www.ingramcontent.com/pod-product-compliance
Lightning Source LLC
Chambersburg PA
CBHW031532040426
42445CB00009B/493